POSTHUMOUS NOON

Also from Gunpowder Press:

The Tarnation of Faust: Poems by David Case

Mouth & Fruit: Poems by Chryss Yost

Shaping Water: Poems by Barry Spacks

Original Face: Poems by Jim Peterson

Instead of Sadness: Poems by Catherine Abbey Hodges

What Breathes Us: Santa Barbara Poets Laureate, 2005-2015

Edited by David Starkey

Burning Down Disneyland: Poems by Kurt Olsson

Unfinished City: Poems by Nan Cohen

Raft of Days: Poems by Catherine Abbey Hodges

Shoreline Voices Projects:

Buzz: Poets Respond to SWARM

Edited by Nancy Gifford and Chryss Yost

Rare Feathers: Poems on Birds & Art

Edited by Nancy Gifford, Chryss Yost, and George Yatchisin

To Give Life a Shape: Poems Inspired by the Santa Barbara Museum of Art

Edited by David Starkey and Chryss Yost

POSTHUMOUS NOON

POEMS

AARON BAKER

GUNPOWDER PRESS • SANTA BARBARA
2018

Published by Gunpowder Press
David Starkey, Editor
PO Box 60035
Santa Barbara, CA 93160-0035

ISBN-13: 978-0-9986458-3-4

www.gunpowderpress.com

Randy B. Baker
1950-2009

ACKNOWLEDGEMENTS

Grateful acknowledgement is made to the editors of the following magazines in which some of these poems, sometimes in slightly different forms or under different titles, have appeared or are forthcoming.

New England Review: "Fairhill Farm," "In Articulo Mortis," "Rife Machine," "Back Forty"

New South: "Highlands Cross"

Ninth Letter: "Cottonwood, "First Language"

Poetry Northwest: "Babel," "The Infernal Regions," "Honeycomb"

Shenandoah: "The New Religion"

Missouri Review: "Dark Matter," "February Nocturne," "Rural Especial Scene," "The Old Nerve," "After"

Mississippi Review: "Late Pastoral"

The Rumpus: "Anax Junius"

32 Poems: "The Shallows," "Deism"

Memorious: "A Field Guide to the Moths of North America"

CONTENTS

I.

Late Pastoral

"'Tis bitter cold. And I am sick at heart." Hamlet

Come, parting dark waves of chlorophyll,
into the last west and the northern woods.
Such a short walk from the meadow, just
a few syllables shifting. Say *eros* without
sibilance, *error*. Thickened shadows, failing
arterial light—now *eternal care* pronounced
internal terror. Vowels pass between
the consonants as wind passes between
the stripped branches. *Forgive* becomes *forgo*.
The afternoon simmers. Blueblossom
and Devil's Club. *Again* becomes *ago*.

February Nocturne

One light burns in a window of the buried house.
Snow-heavy cedars, coyote tracks on the shore.
Our history is not the history of our kind,
or not completely. And nothing is as dull as dying.
I was careless to think that we might be transformed
by one remarkable thing, however small. A maple
leaf, rich red, revolves like a planet beneath the ice.
The heron in last light stands stiff as a spruce
on the bank. Art's failure differs from religion's
in that failure is necessary for it to be itself.
My grandmother used to say, "First I was afraid I'd die,
and then I was afraid I wouldn't." Sitka, Marbled Murrelet,
light fails in the western forest at the foot of the house
of election. What use the madrigals, the may-poles?
Elegy fails unless it ends in resurrection.

Late Night Show

Here in the silence before the poem
is where I've always been, just outside
your awareness. Since before even

you named me, and now I watch
as the nurse comes and goes, as he
trims your nails and sets your hands

back down with unnecessary gentleness.
I've always been here—the shape
of an echo, the pause between words.

Nobody in the barracks knew what to say
when you, the jokester, pulled out
the ultrasound and became suddenly

grave as you showed me around,
the white swirls of my hands, feet,
and head pressing up through the dark.

Now I've returned, ready to speak—
but too late as you fade into the nothing
you coaxed me from. The growing mass

on the slide looks almost familiar,
could be almost a brother. "What's green,"
you once asked me, "and if it falls out

of a tree, it will kill you?" "A pool table!"
On the way back from the clinic in June,
you grew quiet as we drove past the graveyard

on the hill above Sumner. "I can't be buried
here," you whispered. "You know why?"
And this time I got it. "Because you're not dead!"

Headlights on Taft shine through the leaves
of the pear tree. The studio audience
laughs at the monologue on the Late Night Show.

Your breaths are steady, as they have been
for hours. I listen harder for what I've needed
to say. Laughter again, the scattering

of light through the leaves, a faraway
and muffled human noise of call and response.
The curtain stirs. A shoe scuffs in the hall,

more laughter, a car horn. Always
the return of silence, always this need
to trace its form. A new thing will be born.

Dark Matter

We say the heart is sick, meaning something else.
But when we say the body is broken, and it is, the poem,
like a great engine long given up to the weather,
begins to move. Outside, fireweed among the ruins.
We've known the seed of failure in action,
how the worm turns on the root, the foredetermined
uncoiling of the double arms into an electric fizz
and last black sputter of cosmic flatulence. Dark matter:
you take the air, I kick the walls, answer the accusations
to an empty room, then sit down to sob amidst the bones.
It starts to rain. You're elsewhere. *Curse god
and die.* We grow artful when evil, and broken, take
on the utmost of our powers. The garden withers
with such August, but its energy flows inward and flowers.

In Articulo Mortis

1

The enemy descends through the trees and rises through water.
The March wind ripples the lake—opening salvos in the war
against winter. The pulse slows. The hours open.

Soon you will be presented with the enemy's demands.
Soon there will be a journey through a dark forest—every story
you have been told of such journeys represents this one.

Strength needs weakness. That is the story of salvation,
as well as the story of every depravity. Kids, hold hands.
We're going to outdo ourselves this time.

You are as delicate as a dried leaf in the hand, and as ready for fire.

2

The orchard is overgrown, the fence rails splitting at the yard edge,
moss taking hold of the shingles. Painted gnomes portend in the garden,
axes on shoulders, eyes weird among the early blossoms.

Love is the serpent's breath. The bottom of the window box
has collapsed, roots desiccated and dangling. The lab reports
don't mention it, but you disappear behind rows of numbers
and take nothing from this great labor that you can carry in your hand.

The enemy makes you lie down beside still waters. The enemy makes
his face to shine upon you. Love is the whispering in adjoining rooms.

3

Love is the whispering in adjoining rooms, but the enemy won't play
children's games: You say, *My nose. My eyes.*
My mouth, and touch them in turn. The enemy says *Your corpse*

and touches it once. Your wit won't save you now. Nor has faith
healed you. Nor will this matter again except to these few.

There could have been less suffering, said the doctor. *I've rarely seen worse*
because of the situation with the spine. But it could be worse.

I inexplicably pity him as he tells me how.

The enemy is not uninterested in your moral understanding—but many things
beside it pass through his vision. And this although he knows your body
like a lover. And this although he has kept you in the light.

By toil and grief, you will secure your bread. The bologna
you'll have to pick up at Pathmark. You see that the patient is not without
humor. After losing seventy-five pounds he orders a t-shirt

that says *Ask me about my diet plan.* The enemy has sharpened

his knives. He is intentionally vague. Or perhaps
it is not intentional and he is preternaturally calm. He's willing to wait

for you to grow less panicked. You could mistake such patience for indifference.
Frantic efforts have been made. And careful preparations.
But finally it's all just crashing through branches at midnight.

The enemy may not come until you call him friend.

4

You should notice fewer things and dwell on larger themes—
were you to think on them, you would be undone by questions of scale.

The massive meaning of one ragged fingernail,
a spoon leaning in an empty bowl beside a full glass of water.

5

The patient is in-extremis. We move through his death, inhale
it on waking. The enemy will not pass on information.

You know too much already. There does not seem at first to be continuity.
But the indignities accumulate according to a discernable logic.
Some of this is understood by medical science,

some muttered about in the conclaves, some intuited when the breeze shifts
or when light falls a certain way through the closed blinds of a dark room.

One morning, something we've never seen before:
five elk at the pond, two of them wading among the cattails.
Their breath steams as they raise their heads.

It is impossible to die at home, or within any concept.
The nerves are stripped, and then the bones. There aren't stages to grief.

To be cruel, one must be capable of mercy. So the enemy is not cruel.
But finally the enemy shows mercy, and is therein cruel.

6

The currant bushes have spread by the porch. Such bitter berries.
Black landscaping plastic is exposed in places washed out by two winters

of neglect. The cat chases a tuft of cottonwood spores
across the lawn. Breath held within a world of wind. Show me how to die.
Coyotes howl over the hilltop. The cat licks his paws. Smell of honeysuckle.

7

Early on, what the patient hates more than the pain is your pity.
Finally he hates only the pain.

Half asleep, he snatches at his gown. *They do that*, the nurse says.
My mother: *Who are they?* Your thoughts travel widely

but you are not a moving target. Wrench to the instant all of your attention:
there may a chance to culminate in some tiny, some heroically futile gesture.

8

The enemy gives. You can take it with philosophic calm or blubber
over your bucket, but you take and the enemy gives.

Simultaneity and growing, unbridgeable, distance.
There are no meaningless events as the meanings become less apparent.

You've spent too much time at college. Not all problems
are problems of form. Nevertheless, the enemy will grin
at you only in your instances of inexplicable glee.

9

Sign the forms. The devil is in the details, but what else will you have to accept if you believe it? A joke, obviously, and even the dying are wise to simile. Wise as trees. Wise as buckets of whale fat in a bordello.

You are finally you, having been every version of yourself but one. Any moment before the last is not yours, and then the last is not yours.

Spring at the window. Geese on the lake, tufts of pollen swirling upwards.

The patient is concerned by the spiritual lessons you might discern in his suffering. The patient is no longer lifting his arms.

February Nocturne II

Too much talk, too much wind twisted
around in the mouth. I'm not always a liar—
sometimes it's just play, same as silence.
Let fire have its say. Flames walk around
in their circle of stones. Against
the alders, our shadows hunch like smudges
on the wall of a cave. A seen image
won't lie unless you try to glean
its meaning. To mention the moon
is to not only lie but to risk a cliché.
Look: we're together there in our bodies.
Water slaps the dock. The clouds blot
out Polaris. The afterthought's nearly always
the discovery—the owl says who. The moon
rides the blade of the shore into sleep.
I'm still here. The moon blinks,
shadow-crossed, the spider passing over.

Three Lines from Stevens

It must be abstract—

Dose me. Laid out like pinned butterflies,
they rock back their chins
in the terminal ward. Can they hatch
new life from their throats? Variations
on a theme—yes, of course. We float
down the river of ice. Dose me again: time
for the most common profundities.
I too could become—and sometimes am—
a mindless object for another's contemplation.
The Seattle rain comes at the window
sideways and blears my reflection.
I've got part of this down: there's always
someone to bring the needle,
to circle the blue hours
with wings at their shoulders
through a song like the coldest of winds.

It must change—

I am able to hold perfectly still
for hours while remaining in motion.
Funny thing: I dream, and what I dream
is exactly what I see when I wake.
"Are you comfortable, dad?" I've slept
in this chair for a week, afraid even
to slip out for a styrofoam cup of hospital soup.

It must give pleasure—

"Are you comfortable, dad?" But he's not here,
and I'm not either. We move easily
upon the frozen surface, the river bottom

gliding below. Sand and little stones.
A chill breeze, prisms of light drifting
around us. A better breath. A newer sleep,
the almost perfect clarity of thoughtlessness.

Babel

In the end, the things themselves were only descriptions,
globs of light, approximations swimming
up through the eye, and it made us sad to look at them—

Mount Rainier's high Valhalla of ice and stone, glacier fields
and rivers falling through sunlight scrubbed clean by altitude.
On the drive between Paradise and Longmire, we saw

as Percy Shelley did in the Vale of Chamouni
the awful beauty of magnitude. *It's pretty*, she said.
Lower down the Nisqually Basin, the second growth pines,
the meadows of tall grass, seed-heavy and bowing.

———————

A woman I loved now lives in Ohio, and it isn't
the girl who sits reading under the tree on the shore

below that stuns me with my memory of her
but the illumination of late afternoon passing
through the leaves and filling my window.

There shines my writing desk. There shines my chair.

———————

The sin of Babel was the common language, a narrowing
of distance between word and thing—shadow
and light—that brought us nearer to the damnation

of utterances. But say something you don't know already?

Among the cedars just off the highway,
a few rusted out, mossed-over drums lie a-jumble

behind a collapsing woodshed. As the scene comes into view,
you'll see a roofless cabin set further back
in the bottom, burnt timbers and blasted out windows.

The failure's now human in scale, the directives familiar.
Come, said the angels, *let us scatter
their language or they will become like gods.*

———————

The poem denies its materials like the soul denies the body,
and vice versa, but the things still all ask to be emblems,
the newspaper scraps in the gutter, the dented pillow,

my father's wedding ring and stopped watch in a drawer,
and of course somewhere the sculptures, a hundred museums worth,
an entire paradise of gods in which no one believes.

The sirens scream up Sheridan. Lake Michigan pounds
the rocky shore of Fargo Beach. Emergency's in the air.

———————

Finally far enough out, I pull up. The oars creek
in their locks and water slaps the boards. The black
expanse rippling, the city lit up against the continent.

How pretty. What a thing we've made here of steel, glass,
and fire. I miss you terribly! Whatever words are I'd cross
over them into the filial conflagration of so many souls.

———————

After my father's final sermon, an old woman told us
that as he spoke she'd seen angels
holding him up under each arm.

I smiled and thanked her. I hadn't seen angels
and now can't remember a word that he said.

Were I to retell this, I'd restore the catastrophe,
undo the work of the angels, make the sermon
about love, what it demands and does to us.

I'd let the lost meanings, little prodigal sons,
come home and lie down, not let the width

of a breath between the verb and the noun.
Three times the Lord refused the devil on the hill
and still he wouldn't turn the desert stones to bread.

Hell is what happens between my hand and my head.

Rural Especial Scene

Having fallen, having fallen into grace, the servant of god
crawls onto his lawn. Having fallen into grace, his wife
pursues. She calls for their son... Three months later,
I'll stroll across the grass like Huck with rod and reel.
In the pond, those black two acres, the bass begin to breed.
Green surface light and overhead blue. How incongruous
now, that dark encroachment, the day he left the house
for good, twelve tumors like apostles in his head.
This already tedious, this predictable, this vegetable stirring
of first spring after death, this green and posthumous noon.
And metaphor—the real or unreal soul—the mechanical
reflections. What is that rotting in a hole? Stranger still,
I find the needle he tore from his chest and threw
before the paramedics came and covered him where he clawed
the mud, trembled and turned blue. Two months
past care and cure, the bent and dirty needle like a lure.

Water-Strider

Though winged, he walks
            on water.
Skates between elements,
skitters like thought
            through the cattails.
A snake slips unseen through the underbrush.
The forest shifts and sighs, once again
        won't speak its secret.
Between the trees, my father glides
through sunlight, then shadow.
        Surface tension:
the strider rows forward
with middle legs, steers with back legs,
           grasps with forelegs the insect
on which he feeds.
Leaning into my reflection,
        my arched body is the fulcrum on which
all of this turns. The sun hollows the air, burns
it of all but the most essential sound.
Mud-slurp and leaf-stir.
And there, a contrail over the Cascades, the quick
      stroke of a master's hand,
and through the high hush, the vessel itself
     an insect-spark
         on the burnt-in blue.

Rife Machine

Morning's work done, attention curdles—is this pleasure?—into something
remote, a phantom erotic of humidity and exercised, now resting limbs.
How the body, the landscape, finds one vibration and for awhile, hums.

Is it the mind that goes heavy and then the arms, or the arms first
and then the mind? Virginia's drenched swelter of August settles behind the
eyes, an anesthesia of cicadas, the mist-lines of hilltops growing more distant.

Hums – hums as Royal Rife heard it, discredited quack who believed if you found
the right radio frequency, tumors and viruses would literally be shaken and die.
In his last months, my father held the glass globe, lightning arcing within it,

and placed it to his head, his spine, his chest, in the dark room, Bible on his lap
as he fiddled the knobs of the box, polished wood like a radio of the 1940s,
where he looked for the frequency, the broadcast between worlds

that would return him to his life. In between sky and hilltop, cicadas again,
then silence, all kinds of sleep, the disordered murmurings of light. Listen
for that nervous and voluble confluence, that harmony that almost coheres

beneath hearing. Wake, sleep, and wake again. The sun climbs the hill.
Are there words for this music? Listen for what you need. Try harder
to hear that motion within the folds of light. You will be destroyed.

The Infernal Regions

Relax. No more the thinness of ceremony.
Largemouth bass at the bottom of Kapowsin Lake
grow still as his thoughts. No swish and silt,

no father and flail. And once perfectly still, they grow
even stiller. Nothing's wasted, says the Lord of the Underworld.
Stillness is economy, and economy exchange.
While he could still speak, my father asked,
"How should I pray for you?"

The curled buds of the bracken fern form
a forest of question marks.

————

The backhoe operator shuts it down, raises two fingers
towards me and walks off in the rain. Dad's settled
in for the ride, easy now in his pressed suit

and polished shoes. Heavy drops dimple
the freshly-turned dirt. Rainbows of oil in the puddles.
What's left is centuries of silence, such perfect repose.
And potato-salad back at the pot-luck.

————

Should we look for Orpheus among the living?
Should we look for Orpheus among the dead?

Father of riches. Seed the soil, smelt the ore.
We've put on our work boots. We've crossed into

mythology, crossed over. In the underworld,
grief is poor currency. Beneath the camas prairies,

the second-growth Douglas Fir and three bodies
of water, an Atlas of darkness shoulders a weightless

world of light. In the underworld, grief is the only
currency, and music after prayers.
Said Archimedes, "With a long-enough lever
and a place to stand, I will move the earth."

II.

Back Forty

I feel fine. Light vibrates in the branches of the bastard growth.
Feathered shadows of bracken fern. Oregon Grape
and bug-bitten trillium.
                     I've started to think about the problem
of reconciling the eye to the ear, but that smell's whatever's dead
in the underbrush—and overripe blackberries.
Ants fumble noisily at the backlit, finely serrated tips of the hydrangea.

Here is the land I come back to so I can always be going out
from my father's house. When I held him in his last throes,
what I said again and again was, "I've got you,"
as if I was a spotter and the whole thing was some daredevil stunt.

To go forward through music is to work backwards from an idea.
What's met in the marsh is what's meet in Mortality's
mansion. What do you mean by forgiven?
             Pluck out an eye rather than enter the Kingdom
of Abstraction. Strike off an ear rather than give up a savior.

The Shallows

The bluegills drift among the green globs
of frog spawn. The snake rasps awake
in the ferns, a sleepy uncoiling, a motion
meditative in the drift of late August,
late afternoon. In even these tiniest stirrings,
the momentum of millennia—adaptation,
selection, survival. Mindless, undirected,
and mostly error, evolutionary dead-ends
folded into the muck again and again.
Sweet huckleberry, then swamp rot
as the breeze changes through the cattail stalks.
Ammons wrote "There is no finality of vision,"
and "tomorrow another walk is another walk."
I find a stick at the base of an alder and turn over
a squirrel that fell from a hawk. We will
do this forever—a summer sky with clouds
crawling over it and one open eye where sits
without twitching a single black fly.

Cottonwood

Now the first snows of summer, a hot breeze
from the swamp rolling the clumped spores
over the lawn. *Cottonwood*, a word that billows
softly, then falls sharp as a knock on the door.

What do you know about the cottonwood?
It stands among the alders at the lake edge.
Its wood is soft, wet, slow to season, and then
flashes out in the fire like sugar on the tongue.

Cotton-mouth, cotton tail. Copperhead.
Slink along the margins of the bastard growth.
If a thing's not what it's called, how can you
trace your way back from a lie?

When a child opens her hand, says *Look*
and you reach for what's there, she'll snatch
it back and say *You look with your eyes.*
One hot morning, you come onto the porch

in your hospital gown, and what you know
is that the cottonwoods have bloomed,
and beyond what can matter again, released
themselves into the swell and riptide of summer,
the earth itself exhaling, snow in the updraft.

The New Religion

Apostle of Douglas Fir, apostle of pine.
The new religion will have a lot to do
with the rusted bodies of old cars in the woods.
When the last forest has left on the last freighter
bound for Japan, the boss, the bull of the woods,
his name gone to live with his descendants,
will haunt his stripped, shot-out Studebaker
parked in the blackberries on the shore
of Lynch Creek. During the war, even the loggers
taped up the top halves their low-beams—
and blacked-out the fire-roads in the forests.
But now, Lord, we're not on company time.
We're not on anybody's time. We're drunk
on decay. We love our neighbors like ourselves,
and love what we've made, the good steel
of our hearts corrupted by weather,
the rims' last bits of rubber burning
on a road to nowhere, shattered glass
on the backseat, centipedes nestled into the ticking.

Anax Junius

You're sweet. Forget me quickly, that falling and rising over a sea
of baked chlorophyll, swamp-gas filling our wings, our hearts of mud
will sooner spark and flare out their one time as given. I've little interest
left in my body—leg clatter, wing-splay, splatter of light when I love you.
Broken down September, light's loose coins in the marsh grass...we have
12,000 eyes? Did you know that? I did not know, come to this place,
that languor had undone so many. Cold wind—hot wind—
this had everything to do with sex until it became about dying.

A Field Guide to the Moths of North America

Promethea

Midsummer vibrato. Nightfall of yellow
poplar, spicebush and sassafras. Sex
at altitude will end in the underbrush.
Our next subject: the moon.

Luna

All day you horded your shadow,
but at dusk, the spider web
in the low branches of the birch caught
and held, for an instant, the sun.

Grape Leaffolder

I lie curled in the leaf, antennae to yesteryear.
The joy of not-to-be-seen rivals the joy
of not-to-have-been. I missed you this morning,
light-long and blinding horizon. And wind,
wind infinitesimal at the base of the stalk
where passes through dreaming the noonday
thunder of the marching ants' hooves.

Three-banded Fairy

Arrest and suspension. Pasture
and cloud band, one moment frozen
in the sepia light of the 1970s,
a lakeshore, a blanket spread on the grass
and the smell of smoke from a camp fire.
Could you wake now, it would be resurrection.
A flutter, a stir. Your mother's hair.
Your father's voice. A word
whispered out of the dirt.

Virginia Ctenucha

I'll begin within you, your smallest darkness.
Saints are destroyed by their ecstasy, such exuberance
as mine. The cells divide. I squirm in the loam.
The cells divide again! My wings!
A tiny breath unsettles the dust. Then rupture,
metastasis. Metamorphosis in May.

Salt Marsh

Just a scrap of white silk in the clover.
A gentleman will wear a white
bow tie after nightfall for the most formal
occasions—an inauguration perhaps,
or the sinking of an ocean liner.
Shall we fly or shall we feed?
Think of me fastened at your dead father's throat.

Darling Underwing

I'm a broken chip of bark, the skeleton of a leaf,
whatever's left-off and useless, and anyway, Lord,
you're already glutted on the Autumn smoke of burning
bodies. Turn your face from me. A loving father
won't spare the rod, but I'm fatherless and past
correction. These colors help me hide.

Yucca

The meanest flower that blows, and day wombed
in its underfolds. The thing I've waited my whole life
to tell you can now go unsaid. Lowly, lovely, love.
Forestall. Wait for me on your side
of the morning. For now, a marvel in the meadow:
the last light twists on a single petal's edge.

Carolina Sphinx

A dying grub. What's lowlier than pupating
inside this desiccated shell? I'm an amputated
digit in the dirt, nectarivorous at night.
I hover with remarkable stillness above the flowers
on headstones—drink those
severed currents. All night the dead flutter past
your window on thousands of wings.

American Dagger

So serious, son. A little tact, a little circumspection—
try not to head straight for the flame.
Eventually it's the slow burn
of aftermath anyway, the occasional return—

the play of light, a step in the dance, a certain silly song.
As you fly home for Christmas, it's John Denver
and a bag of peanuts, dusk over Colorado,
red snow-streaks on the summits.
You can talk to God and listen to the casual reply.

Webworm

I'm coiled deep in the skittery
paper-shuffle of communal life.
Sententious, my hair
parted behind. And though dull as you please—
the white hallway, the pleasantries
exchanged in the elevator—
I'll wait long enough to lap
your blood from a leaf.

Coddling

The bottom-line: you'll never come first.
The theme is need and I devour. Apple, walnut,
pear—O sad suburbia! O grim internia,
distant dawn! Who'll be with us in the round
of our need? Who'll be left to draw the curtains?
Who'll be left to mow the lawn?

Common Sheep

Who are you that moves among these shades?
Aaron, come off it! Here we are at the swamp's edge,
and here are the salmonberries. See the cattails?
Pull one from the mud. Wipe the frog-spawn
and strip it to the stalk. The root tastes like cucumber.

Silver-spotted Ghost

I fly unseen through your interstices
of expectation. And with no love
for the lights of the living.
Glimpse me if at all sidelong and streamside
at dusk. Then meet me again just past
the lines of your own disappearing.

Clouded Crimson

Night again. Catechisms of unasked questions and ungiven answers.
Want death to be the fallacy—and dream? Or the dream
to be the fallacy—and death? Refrain.

Fall Cankerworm

Refrain. At last the marvel and the terror, the wordless You.
Be still. The new muscles twitch. The wings scrape at the shell.

Object Lesson

The remembered world—at dusk the cardinal
a red explosion among the mimosa's pink splatters.
Too much altitude, too much of this unfolding
of shadow and sound, high romance on suburbia's
margin. But I do like the smell of burning charcoal
and meat wafting from the neighbor's grill, and know
her a little better now as night settles in, the spider
with her swollen sac traversing the aluminum frame
of the screen, rounding the edge to get away
from the porch light burning in the cobwebbed glass.

Fairhill Farm

Caffeinated daybreak, ridge-line over the porch rail.
What glides at eye-level above the creek bottom,
surveilling the pasture? Peregrine Falcon? Harrier?

The world charged like shook foil—that's a good one.
Its colors sharpen as we come out of the inbetween.
Wind-gusts rattle these pages, empty interiors, room enough

for any grief you'd fill them with. And what are we calling this—
exile?—and what's wrong with you anyway?

Elms line the shore, knots of aspen on pasture and hillside.
Granite and clay, buzzing shade and moving water.

What else can inhabit a secret place from afar—
what else would try? The Black Rat Snake
has something to tell you. No he doesn't. When you survive,

it won't be like the Five-Lined Skink does,
the Loggerhead Shrike or the Prairie Wobbler.
Are you getting this down? Look and go on looking, you
with your clean hands, your hurt, and mellifluous dawn.

———————

Fade-lines—memory's green vistas, its blue vistas
and stonescapes. Its drawn shades and unwashed
dishes. Careful kiddo. Being too honest is its own

kind of lie. Why does a summer's day
need at its center some Lady of Walsingham,

some placidity where you can crawl on your knees
with the penitents? *In the midst of mystery*

you pass by yourself without wondering.
Mid-afternoon. Vibrato of insects, Blue Ridge
to the west, Atlantic to the east. A porch. A deck chair.

———————

August's divisions, pasture from forest,
birdsong from silence. Darkness leans

harder against the light, a furious last flowering
in the margins, and evening as perfumed and desperate
as the sweaty last slow dance at the end of prom.

Ridge from ravine, aftermath from harbinger.
Mull it over, but you've got bigger problems now
than the profound. Seen at this distance,
the cars on South River Road pass but don't make a sound.

———————

Grounds and occasion. One glass,
sliced tomatoes shining in vinegar,
blackened bits of rosemary on the blade.

Cattle steam in the pasture below. A dog-run deer
lies half out of the creek. Wind through the aspens
unveils it like a seductress's thigh. The bottle's still
half full, the evening filled with nothing.

Knife and fork, knife and fork, the napkin folded
carefully on my knee. Father's gone, she's gone.

Satieties rebel as bodies rebel—as language

follows our bodies. The meat is best by the bone,
the fat cut by the cabernet's bite. The livestock
go on masticating in the high grass. What's the worry?

The turkey buzzards arrive and things get
smaller, then smaller still to become full-featured
microcosms that nothing worms out of.

How abstract, this winged circling around
what once gave pleasure and will give pleasure again.

The Old Nerve

Fitting sacrifice: again the pig, his viscera dragged
steaming beside water streaming through Precambrian light.
Where there was none, we made love.
Where there was none, made religion, then said *too much*,
too much as the smell of burnt fat filled our nostrils.
Slick the blade, turn the spit. Even kinship is cruel,
always another to leave us behind
like a coat caught in the harlot's hands.
We can never be brutal enough for this world.
You said God is the spark of the divine in another.
You said where there's smoke there is fire.
But let's decide some other time if there's fire where there's fire.
Good eyes, mellifluous tongue! Legs, how you've grown!
Gristle beneath the nails, sizzle of green wood in the pit.

News Hour

Begin anywhere. Falling indicators, rising indicators,
the bomb that went off in the square, a stump
of an Alaskan Cedar at the bottom of an overgrown

orchard. Gray sawdust and termite droppings spill
over the trunk, withered apples among the clover
and crabgrass. Let's be clear—these debts

won't be repaid. It's noon, you're alone,
smells of scorched grass and blackberries.
Another bomb—the Dow reacts. Take a little

sawdust in your hand. It's damp and clumps
as it sifts to your boots. Probably, you've been
more fundamentally wrong than wronged,

and probably I said to be nice. As I wrote this,
a feral cat dragged a dying cottontail under
my window. I stood to look and she ran, but then

three kittens appeared and started pawing at the rabbit.
After awhile, the mother returned and lay
side-by-side with the rabbit's body as the kittens

suckled. I have something to tell you.
Are you still in the woods? Meet me if you can
at the second gate halfway up the pasture.

III.

Another Screwball Comedy

Too many poems with moons in them.
Too many sidewalks, dead grandparents, birds.
Too much of that feeling you gave me—
any of us can be put aside. Someone
on the sidewalk is shouting in German.

Too many poems in German.
Too much waking up and going back to sleep.
Too much of the wind off Lake Michigan
blowing the lids from our trashcans.
Too many guitars luring the moon out of the lake.

And again as always, too much of the lake,
of your attention and lack of attention.
I'm thinking about the small of your back
pressed into my palm. I'm embarrassed
to say say so. There is too much

embarrassment in our poems as well
as not nearly enough embarrassment.
Here is what passes for mystery.
Too much eternity before, in, and after
our poems. Too many hymns and homonyms.

If you call now, we won't need to talk.
All night, the sidebars, the urban bards,
the cowl of darkness. All night, a fledgling
Barred Owl crying in the hawthorn over
the sidewalk. *Die ganze Nacht weine ich für Sie.*

Sunday Matinee

1

A pill drops from a plastic bottle into one hand as the other
reaches for a glass of water at the bedside. White sheets,
white walls. Beyond the sill, a crooked windowbox of red peonies.

2

Like the soul captured and wrenched out of time
when a camera's flash explodes and aperture snaps,
a metaphor arrests what should be set in motion.

3

Seen from across the lawn, a red ellipses tilts beneath the window.
Rewind through the window box being nailed there, the raising of walls,
the foundation poured into forms dug into the hillside.

4

Through the hillside forest swelling out of the swamp, through ice retreating,
regathering, and then fast forward again through ice fragmenting,
the swamp, the hill, and in a blink the house again and peonies.

5

A hand raises a pill to the lips and the house crumbles. The forest
climbs over it and the hill sinks into the swamp. The film unspools, slips,
slaps the reel, and at last: a clean white light upon a blank white sheet.

Bitterroot Range

Just another day of muddling around in my corporeal
form. Far below, the Clark Fork glitters toward
its vanishing point. The Wild Horse Plains lie half-swallowed
in the shadow of the Bitterroot Range. I always misunderstand
things the the first time around, the great absences
seeming more tolerable than the small ones, and a mild
evening in a summer without you the least tolerable of all.
In the gulley, the twig-gathering wren's song mocks
the night birds where they brood, their great wings
folded over their eyes. If we could pass from argument
to description, could we be restored to perfection,
and not speaking follow the creek even further next time
into the hills? Of course, wanting such a thing
was itself our undoing. Gravel-crunch and smell
of sage. Far below, the small private lights of houses
lie clustered in the river bend. A few headlights appear
on the highway as men begin to clock out of the mills,
wipe sawdust from their boots and head for home.

First Language

Before a spirit enters a body, it moves unfixedly
    through the forest, is light dappled over stones,
is floating fern spore in the peripheral vision

        of the still or already living. The black
eye of the Varied Thrush continues to rove.
        The centipede extends its scintilla.

Go on looking for your points of entrance,
        of purchase and leverage.
 Go on believing that you will heft the weight

        of your unreality onto the real.
Before meaning enters a language, it moves.

        Go on listening, watching, and waiting to be born.
The shape stirs beneath the sheet.
        The light sifts the listening stones.

Deism

And the sun drifts down the day like a floater in my left eye,
      all these spheres within spheres,
clock and compass, all the little cogs catching,
      corpuscles and organelles churning,

the stars themselves following their mapped routes
      of rotation around us,
sweep of the protractor defining each diurnal course,
      heavenly bodies wound up to whirl
around an eye placed at the center
      of an illuminated chart with an overlaid graph.

Right. Wound up like a clock to run while the creator ran off
      to Antigua. Bodies in motion, his banner over me is love,
and love, here's looking at you. Looking harder as we listen and think.
      Our gazes lock. God blinks.

After

After the seven sheddings of blood
and the traitor's kiss, after the cock's third crow
and the prayer in the garden, after the torn veil
and the mid-day midnight, I put on my Adidas.

I put on my Adidas like the armor and sword.
After the third day of the broken body.
After the ruptured seal and the rolled-away stone,
I shake the milk carton. I wait at the bus-stop.

After the stained shroud and the dusty footprint,
after the rumors muttered by locusts, after
the calm settling over the waters, I write my name
on the back of a VISA. After the voice

from the smoke. After the pillar of fire by night
and the prophet's shorn beard. After the lamb's
blood on the door post, I wait for the phone call.
I pass through the turnstile. After the wars

and the rumors of wars. After Ruth crying in the fields
for her children. After the midnight knock on the door,
I update my profile. I apply for the permit.

After the hand dipped in water, I keep my place in the line.
After the ninth generation, after thirty pieces of silver.
After the seventh sign and the second-born son.

The Deaths of Others

It happens like their good looks,
their wisdom I cannot acquire,
even their ignorance. I stand
outside but am myself the measure.
How casual it ends up being after
a lifetime of hymns. The eyelids
fluttering, gazes turned to the wall,
the long exhalations they exit on.
Someone leaves a room and everyone
goes on talking. I pick up a glass
of water, and when I put it down
empty, it's been moved a half inch.

North Shore

1

The hands sweep round the hours, July in full motion,
the toplit and then the underlit trees. Afternoon
in undulation, leaf and grass blade in slow stir and etched

relief. The day's still searching for its subject,
but the stage is set and adequate for anything.
Behind wrought-iron gates, long lawns meander

down to the lake. Laughter and the smell of grilled meat
spill from the park. The cars regatta down Sheridan Avenue.
A dog barks. Take it all in, each part unparsed, assimilated,

and washed through with sunlight. Here is a pause that continues,
a pause you could live in, your life of pure sensation.

2

Listen: sometimes the point is the digression.
The larger act justified by the smallest gesture.
Remember this when what's worked before is failing—

that good hocus pocus of the faraway wrenching
the nearby into focus. Between these high and low blues
of sky and water, the gull's wings flail against the wind,

and the maker's voice, such as it is, can barely

portion out the shore. There's Chicago's skyline to the south,
so much glass aglitter, and here, goldfinches
back from Mexico hanging out in the honey locusts.

3

Then autumn sets its tooth and summer's bathers walk home
a little earlier, adults with arms folded against the chill
looking suddenly philosophical, sullen children trailing

their towels. The storm comes in. Dusk electrifies
the mist line over the lake. The black mass of cloud suspended
above water coils and uncoils as it writhes toward us.

4

So there it is. Decades it's taken to return to me. I'd nearly forgotten
that evening in a single-prop Cessna stuttering aloft
on the thermals over the Papuan coastline north of Port Moresby,

the highlands rolling away on one side and storm approaching
over the sea on the other. A burning angel in terrible contortion,
the sun aflame between the folding and refolding columns of cloud.

It's still months before the founding of the Chimbu mission,
and I'm learning to read. A blue Hardy Boys book lies open
across my knee. Whatever past seethes in the storm

still isn't mine to remember. When I complain about pressure
in my ears, my mother gives me a stick of gum. When the turbulence

worsens, my father smiles and removes his glasses.
He breathes onto the lenses, rubs them with his shirt-cuff.

5

The subject was always survival. The scene becomes more bare,
sensation cleaner. A cold rain scours the stones on the shore,
the tide-break a long ellipsis of white caps left to right

across the window. I once asked my father how it was possible
not to love the world or the things of the world.
You've got me there.

                    A cup steams on the desk.
The cat lies curled on the rug. And there by the lamp,
a half circle of hand-written pages.
Here's home, and the danger's now the inner life,

that counterpoised warmth. This morning is of the world.
In the revised draft, dried leaves scribble down Jarvis
in the wake of a garbage truck. An El runs between

the Gold Coast and Goose Island. I mean an L lies
between the world and the word. This morning's of the world.
Of the fog over the lake. Of the clean linens folded on the shelf,
of the ice webbing the corner of the window glass.

6

At the cornices, gargoyles stare into winter ever-more-widely
as their eyelids erode. Time has weathered your wings,
made dogs of you.

                                At my writing desk, I lean with you toward
the east and hope for one glimpse...one glimpse...
Below you a sign reads: VINTAGE APARTMENTS.

What would you fly from? Forgive us. It was just a story
we told ourselves, your horns and your talons. Go to sleep,
go to sleep, we forgive you.

No one actually expected you to burst from the stone
and soar into the mists on Lake Michigan.

The wind continues its work, keeps its secret—
how the story will come round at last and be set right
without us. It's correct that I should continue to labor below you.

Correct that you should dissolve more lengthily above me,
our bodies so near but still not rising,
still not turning so far as we know into sunlight or song.

Highlands Cross

I'll wake upon my white sheet when I'm saved.
My third rib ached. But then I learned to sleep.
River breezes stalked the moonlit rows

of coffee trees along the mission's yard.
I'll tell you this the day that I am found:
memory was the light cupped in my palm.

When I was lost, I carried it like home.
Smoke rose above the villages at dusk
and scents of flowers settled in my hair.

The Highland chapel's cross is standing still.
I watched you raise it when I was child
and the landscape rose to meet it on the hill.

Believe the ways I've found to take it up.
Its little fire warmed me through the north,
but as I grew it wanted all my strength.

Now morning waits for just a single word.
You said a spirit moves upon the deep
and every son is recognized at home.

What is this place? And who is at the door?
I feel the seasons turn from wet to dry.
I train my hands to turn a single stone.

California Coastal

How would it be to inhabit the lives of others—
not to redeem them but ourselves? Put them on
at first in their gentlest incarnations

as they appear in airports, subways, or mildly bored
in line at the supermarket?
                              I move like an afterthought
through the storm, float through the jetstream

out of Chicago's worst winter in decades and connect
through LA. At last the turboprop shudders, descends,
and touches down in San Luis Obispo

as if in the afterlife, an evening of mandolins
and the celebrated heraldic scent of lilacs.
My fellow passengers move unhurriedly
over the tarmac with that tanned affluent ease
of Coastal Californians.
                              Think of us arriving
seaside to sit in white shirts and sip Chardonnay
under the pepper trees as evening simmers over the Pacific.
How genial we must seem to you, and unapproachable.
Still, it is exhausting to travel by air,

and when we look up at it afterwards, the sky seems as suddenly
empty as a hospital bed. What's behind is sad and difficult,
a test successfully passed that has weakened us in ways

we can't yet fully know. The propellers sputter and stop.
The baggage handlers wrestle bags from the hold.
A sense surrounds us now of a dormant sensuality.
It's said a knowledge of god is impressed on each of our hearts.

The Unnaming of the Animals

Now we will unname the animals, now pry from our speech
the syllables that have kept them from the garden.

I cannot say what moves there, the quick tongue flicking
over the fangs, the green eyes aglow in the underbrush,
the hush that falls over the forest as the predator arrives.

Because silence means danger, something might yet survive,
might yet feed in the garden. Now we will unname the animals,

return to the impulse one remove from original sin.
I do not mean original error or mean to say some name
of god that might draw a word nearer to its incarnation.

To name a thing is to claim it, the silver splash in the water,
the cry in the alley, the wing angling into the wind.

To so much as cast out a devil, you must call it by name.
The hiss, the fur beneath your hand, the tail curled
along the back of a sleeping body—let us begin now

to unname the animals! Our father calls out in the garden.
No one answers and he must think us ashamed in our nakedness,

but now we are naked even of our names. Now we release
the animals from our dominion. Let the sheet enfold
and return them to the sky—the stamping hoof, the slashing

claw, the grunt and the feather. We must release them,
release them all that we might unfix and fall out of time.

Rock Island Lines

Then one day, green again and crystalline April,
birds filling the honey locust at my window.
How did I fail to notice—and what's this
the blood remembers and rises to tell?
Star-crossed—no—the sun has crossed
each of March's Maginot lines, and just
like that I'm conquered, a good morning's work.
Anger was good animation and ennui a scratchy
scarf and sweater to snatch at like the dying snatch
at their gowns, but now death has gone a little senile
in the sapless elm, now the Mississippi has receded
behind the flood walls. Now birdsong, now a little
time at least to pick over whatever's been
cast up on the floodplain. The sun leans hard
against Rock Island, morning mist at the shoreline,
the vaporous cross-outs, spring revising the manuscript.

Late Pastoral II

Sky and field. Nowhere touching, we make a horizon.
You hold a lake that holds me, admire my scope and I your
variety. *Camas, buttercup, groundhog, sage. Cirrus, false dawn,
funnel.* But my rage always dies—now nothing disturbs our mutual
contemplation. Soon something. June-gentle. Wind westerly. Goldenrod.

Honeycomb

Here is the dream where dust, gathered and blowing over the field,
    turns suddenly against the wind and moves with the shape
of a body. Here the shape of a body forms and reforms as it crosses
    the sky, and then you hear it, the hum of the swarm,

the resurrection of the will heard first by the forest saints who fashioned
    skep-baskets of mud, dung, and straw to draw, hold,
and harvest it. The black globes of the bee's eyes regard you

as the earth does, which is barely at all, an unflowering stalk
    in the field. In April, you are no Oregon Grape, Willow, or Cottonwood.
In May, no Poison Oak, Buckbrush, or Vine Maple. Here are the stacked
    hives in the glade, row and white row of return.

Saint Augustine declared evil an absence of good. But an angel guards the gate
    back to the garden. Good is an absence, and here below

her gaze, life rises from the dust, root conspiring with raindrop, flower
    with stamen, these tiny messengers passing secrets
between them. Soon now, autumn will arrive, the emergency be upon us.

Soon the combs will overflow with honey. Soon we pagan priests
must put on our accruements and enter the glade, fill it with the smoke
    of our censers, bewilder the bees and blind the eyes of the angel.

About the Poet

Aaron Baker's first collection of poems, *Mission Work*, was the winner of the 2007 Bakeless Prize in Poetry and the 2009 Glasgow/Shenandoah Prize for Emerging Writers. A former Wallace Stegner Fellow in Poetry at Stanford University, he received his MFA in Creative Writing from the University of Virginia. He has been awarded fellowships by the Bread Loaf Writers' Conference and the Sewanee Writers' Conference and is an assistant professor at Loyola University Chicago.

CPSIA information can be obtained
at www.ICGtesting.com
Printed in the USA
LVHW040250141118
596829LV00009B/205